gifts

rob mclennan

TALONBOOKS

Copyright © 2009 rob mclennan

Talonbooks
PO 2076, Vancouver, British Columbia, Canada V6B 3S3
www.talonbooks.com

Typeset in Adobe Garamond and printed and bound in Canada.

First Printing: 2009

The publisher gratefully acknowledges the financial support of the Canada Council for the Arts;
the Government of Canada through the Book Publishing Industry Development Program; and
the Province of British Columbia through the British Columbia Arts Council and the Book
Publishing Tax Credit for our publishing activities.

LIBRARY AND ARCHIVES CANADA CATALOGUING IN PUBLICATION

McLennan, Rob, 1970–
      Gifts / Rob McLennan.
Poems.
ISBN 978-0-88922-605-0
      I. Title.
PS8575.L4586G53 2009   C811'.54   C2008-906197-7

Contents

gifts

(for Meredith Quartermain)

.

later on she said that the little things counted
every little thing, they all mattered
he said no, they did not, he said that was a way
to insanity
     — Michelle Desbarats, *Eve'n Adam*

It is not epiphanies we are after
(God forbid!)
but a small truth or two—
     — John Newlove, *THE TASMANIAN DEVIL & other poems*

Yes, and today as I write
I will it to be so, just as you thought.
     — Lori Emerson, *Letter Fragments*

a valentine for _____

was curtain for the rod, a slipper trapline
rain together, if we could rain
dont talk to me
                    were you struck by further
, edge of long world paper soft
                    abt being alone; it could be
songs for soft fishes, it could be
a sandy hill enterprise we never
& then some, but you said it so

what do the knees need, lied for pleasure
of already breached, insufferable
                              ; a longest open door
would velvet & blockade, would freelance sharp taste
& swans port, wings the sport up

clandestine exposed or juxtaposed, writing
a condition of famous last words,
writing the crack in semblance,
the slow root of digression
                    & a patient lung,
riding stropic, now down
otherwise filled

if this left to do or done, one may
legitimately, fable

a valentine for tina-frances

how are network & lost girls divided,
on main street, dancing; the sun come up,
the permanence of condensed milk
& language arts on even spread; *what else*
                    do whiskers;
what else *speed*
            writing days & aches & pattern
left on bicycle locks & up the long-limbed leftovers

            this is a new truth in sacrifice,
we hug our shadows, tight to breathe a *gung-ho*,
what otherwise regard
                    high heels & perfect legs,
would otherwise sew by hand, sending lyric
denim, cotton
                    the limited use of price
& space; if time as literate as touch
a mirror of its own gone lost, gone some remain
        but turn discursive; what else
a stack of pennies open yard

when my shoes hit the floor & gravel drive

white sweatshirt worn & lavender,
a blue dress thinking fits

a valentine for lea

a letter before a letter; thoughts presented go
an island surface nation thin
          "letter writing as poem, practice, praxis"
a new twin thump; prospects
arent everything, a heart in swimming new york
feet on the cold hard floor of maine
                              whos for counting?
a din & an impulse, shirts colour blue
& right for summer, spring
                    a chore of footprints
sand aching mannerisms, ruin
            a bolt across commercial sea & falls fake

the speaker as a wholesale fragment
or seldom constant, a city scoops body brown
& lycra, complements the beach
                    & layers of clothing, wash
then wish: *a moonstruck slap*

you know you as intention stains; a sleeve

why *dont* you wish the white pacific? why
dont you wish the corridor?

a gesture for monty

                 ; bluegrass pluck,
a sugar reel sleeps weekend limb,
a stretch of states & nothing, the world owes
        receding tides; you a limping
set in paper,
            scissors, stone

if selected works regress; imitation bleeds
       an echo; eyebrow
off of henry moore

a reckless, wrecking ball
is tempered action by a virgil burl
       each surgery interprets figures, fawn
a lug to share as proxy; migration lodge
         throughout the coastal, mountain rage

indeed her beauty, a solution
in the grass

the port side seat the wing; or swim
an envelope to shore

a hazard of excavation is the happy wasp
amid the speaking bones

a valentine for jennifer

if struck one, signs a glazed tsunami
gatineau clearances; dots of fruit
      & fly stone slicker; river sticks
translations slip the water drop like gravity
        cats jump go to blossom
quickly; joyful cracks in order

by definition, painted black or painted pink a princess
rooms a rhythm gestures; small to take,
      to fiddle resin up the valley bow
a pontiac stretch; goes valley-wide
& finds
        to once a gut your ground

combination of found & fact & carried
an information slips a mouth, comes
      monumental; melodrama twist

or sparking heat in burnished holes,
third-party worn

& knows of only two positions: this way
& the last

a valentine for emma, two-&-a-half, & rory, newborn

in every day a gesture drops pretension, skin
of crystals rich in notebook flows
a cup I now believe
                              ; white house
on the mantic hill
                    what constructs our flight?
if bedrock sticks too much to lose
, the stone house or the reddened brick, would
        hopelessly neck; a pounce

two sisters new, where sky is big enough above
to share; invisible warmth & what the
                        dog keeps dragging in
a house as safes; the little twigs & skulls
the bush-feeds, wild rhubarb
        & the winter-wasps, feeding names for snow

each morning records a word, another surface
haunting their own halls, if even

whisper in a wet field; dogs
& horses nuzzle

a message for susan

a swans taste, gesture in the thin, plant bath a stretch
would know it then
              a key parenthetical point
or block away is just
          via regular notes & open software, heart
arrhythmia slip; if known held anything back
of interesting fields or hot water tanks in stones

               send out your prophets
vancouver drains of painted days
a brown-backed sofa; a lidless sleep a sheep-count
robbing peter to offer paul
                   ; slowly, a
        terrible distance

momentum in airplanes on mountain
relishing friends & family; *what follows a sampler*

a dream-swipe text

a hieroglyph for victor

what duly flames would answer; tall-boy thin,
or writing france a tongue
                    look throne-ward, tangle
furious constraint of errant cruelties
would testify; a trigger turning
                    silence on its ear
what *about* the carnage? what about
                    the parties for defence?

a crystalline-layered tract; incendiary history,
to what hand surface, swooning, thin-billed chastity
            every kilometre turmoil bags

stop your arm a stimulant; virtues clear
& mutton birds, snakewise standing by toronto
& speak *no previous knowledge* speak

the lake the water swimming at
a victory victor tin man studied
                    , belly-dance medicine

or catch a vacant claim

a fish in stomach scrawls

a semaphore for sheila & reg

in a realm of balcony regard; *what lies across from dream*
could also be considered dream
                                        heightened cortex
mainstream minutes, musical torque
for every lip of cloud desired
                        ; the neighbours bleed & crow,
throw chicken-bones
                                a lighthouse fissure
in there; private definitions still
        of what we knew
against them; walking pulse & step-things

when did the car scars; how long
can an anguished form?

or swim a switching, small
exceeding beauty; a window
                    thinks it smart unseen

two tin-cans waxy string composed

the streets change star to sun to stone

a valentine for kate

dont anyone look at the longest film; a trappers curse,
burn black or red cerulean; *slag burning*
, a man must try to
                              ; try, keep track
           on any hum, a tongue traced
barter in belief; my daughters curls,
almost separate from her, screening options

once there was nothing to do

once there was nothing; a county time wrong
of the year, a schoolboy spins
           out thin & fragment hopes
a good downpour; once into slowing down
; remembering first words, step, a day
                              down teachers looks

calamity claim, no plain-jane; no-nonsense history
& tales told out of class; your mother
                     then for details, *knows*

breaking off these geographic missions
pulling off commissions like a log

where it would be warmer you would never

a valentine for margaret

who could be smartest; nether lengths
of poem writing company *less content*
more constant; view
                          from listen sting-sharp hills
porch what light glistens? the automatic agreement
of children & spotlight, pianos
           as sensitive insect eyes; the stroller
down particular instant sidewalk college
                                would do then
invoke a need; more suitable living

                          or shifting water degree
of grasped into the ground; a baseball mouth
& house we live in
                    finish visits
& picnic tables, not steeds; turns
from the body & spits out an eye-line
from her third

or many-lettered splendour
, pleasing measure

a door not necessarily open left upon

a story for john

if you would; bodies listing, listing in
a slick of heaven-sent, a drinking-art
drives his head down body
                            blows, the chill air
masquerading out; nineteen-eighties rock,
a generational scourge, a piecemeal
foundation-long; *knows*
what knows; his mothers dancing legs
           in black & film white
before any invented him, or siblings long

        one story song a story; the dream
re-tuned to ware; the journey
at the small begin
                go seek
go out & boundary holes; like he does
speaks death-rattle soft
            a wind-shook path & sunk

about as then; through uncolonized boundaries

is lifting up a lake; night after
            answer measured day

      or then

a valentine for amanda

so present & so personal; construction burns
misnomer name, a motorcycle helm, the patty
    duke show; *the stuff we retain*
                    (is mostly water)
would land a stack in shadow, distracted simply
couldnt cure
        furniture isnt everything
a moneyed ramble takes its toll

a light bare basis; in the background
fried domestic, new lover & a casserole
missing tricks
           of speed & sleeve, I havent
said eternal, broken blue-lead glass
umbrella walls in hand
       & sexsmith, ron; a happy page
of breeding *my space* life

if cant seduce, she says, I may as well amuse

or doing so, a fragile bruise of scorched earth
morning glimpses through

: *four corners of the real*

an elopement gift for shane + rebecca

how did you went; an island kingston shack
you fed mosquitoes, bees
       & sprawl the theatre, nature; the body alters,
automatically west, & turns you back
ad nauseum, museum-still; death to every thing, delay
       in dervish hands; *a beautiful*
car parked only;
             festival then,
propose self-evident italian skin
& coffee-song the kitchen view
       a weekend breeds

       is this a limit? longing,
at least; to structure knowing stain
& quiet fields; *of paint*

a gauge-field jealous, still
to bedrock quart the prescott

where spoken never resembles
a flight path out of all

your special wonders

a card for michelle

what shyness breeds; *a habit force*
takes force to bruise; inside these lines, a plane
is pilot noise so white its see-through
       ; *sigh*, the folk-art drains relief
a limb from lifting
                people place you,
cousin second if you know a slow wash
freckles off the page; what topics

          would you claim; a too-much mire
, mine, the arms of old trees nestle
wrench a saddled glebe; *you walk*

, *you blade*
         you roller-smooth
a trestled taste & morsel, fiery small
would automatic shift

or library, the price of words
that mark below you, miracle

of the seeming past; a rapture-cast

    some teenaged leak

I waiting write you, telephone a ferry-tough

a wedding gift for anita + james

would top send torpor; merrickville laugh
of gender-bliss in spades
        & play-thing houses; *would evident, arrange*
& sleep out plain; tan under clouds
                that crept you, swimming
from ste laurence blights

        an old fall eased up squeeze,
a clearer brush would brimful birds
at first a peppering; thousands, know we moved
the landscape green; from brown to this,
              a platter-sleep
      perspective-long & angel-mute

the banks would hem; a love would harken, grow
neglect & butchered, still be some
           & always in the house *I do*

a skidder charge command; *to lay*

to translate any colonies, a hinter
land is land is quickened silence swim

imply more good *impossible*
; is already in *complete* & soldiered

a valentine for carmel

deployment wonders; a stationary two-wheeled psyche
tending two hundred hour kilometres; *sweet*
         is harkened speed; a slew
of regimental bliss
           stuck & strike make plunder,
base for new words to the fore
& lazy battles
         two ships, pass; a classical bent
for sundry, wunderkind, a terrible
concoction of christmas & a sheet of nails

(*but would you*)

       no slater stay, an imposition
       wrapped in captured flags
           or new wave hours
      , letters latter market street

     or not enough original sin

         ; *lines descend like snowflakes*
& carve a public umlaut voice; no metropolitan
space for wonder, sign for a building
or through the waves & little garden stones

an apology for ann-marie

what you always said you wanted; needle red,
a guinness, leonard cohen; tequila thirds,
cranberry sweet & seven-up; my best
           & only, first; *that you would contribute*
struck powerlines, despair built out of straw
& wood, & brass tax, vigour out
             of hard stone; *mention*
never could be mentioned; an island, red
& sand for counting,
                   suddenly real
glen norman made from thinking
                  & absorbed

into your limbness, limits

where; a tribute made to afternoon & evenings,
trembled hard-wired body warm
            & insect only
      in sheer determination

the crack & thistle glowing lily orange
in two hands, a dollar month
         or six short weeks

you didnt say a word

has further gone w/ less or more than never-wrong

a smoke signal for derek

what cowgirl stitch endure; a glitter-mask amusement
days are long & light rail
        plastic letters rearrange
how do become a substitute, writing pages
double newsprint kitchen trays

      a studio lemon, lime; what must be done
is parenthetical; stitch implies progress, jargon
implies narrative a sentence fifteen years
from jar to jar
            how much detail
can bare colour give, addressing envelopes
a meeting; songs a pretty light
                of cowtown, yard
a house fenced in
      or do you think it

a hand a group a tribe the trees to yellow
foothills hand the fingers searching out

      nothing were forgotten to

the name a fake for all these states

      a floating keeping pool

a wake for duncan

what never made; the very same
                distracted listed youth ensure
for fighting interrupted all that meant
               ; *reverend outward,*
a border lead embracing, pint
extended hours schedule irenes afternoon
      of view
                a lansdowne perch,
bled homeward, south
& rising; let a pitch out fundamental
is your god; & where else would a syllable
right princess up, subtraction

                          this cornwall end
dunvegan then; your mother in the log house
bliss directing; sentient for sure,
      a film clip of instant, shrill

& all mankind a score a great emotion

a valentine for clare

slips incognito; plays pan fluke *never-never*
constant watching of linguistic skill an evil laugh
       ; *the limits journey*
kamloops kicks, a cactus hand of fences
home original; the parent of one has blanched,
the parent of two
              runs circles, hidden songs
in breath; a scythe of desert rain
your swordfish, *expert under advice*

       rings & dial tones you busted
grass skirt w/ a comic villain; beer balloons,
back-breaking smile
              swans the constant prose
into a combined will

where endless nights & bryan camps
the mines go wild; costume
    if you see the state; pretend, & thanks, thumbs

still they howl, hit the meadow-rail

       the safest speak in awe

would save a homegrown grief of maps
of new entire continents

a party favour for jerry + jennifer

the backyard bunts a birthday; grand slam of pig,
the roast & turkey deep-fried
        ; *here we are in ages*; soother shot
the theory & practice of censorship; affected zones
                 need little milk, a difference
made of *one strong year*
                   ; split something glass
, was something else to do; your words come
in a frosted cup
             in blue wool dressing,
cars & bicycles, locked frozen in a slingshot box
& *silly soft distinction*
             house breeds
you breeds a house on spruce the new spruce
trickles laneway south
             we all
were regulars, then; a late at long dusk,
smart cheese & flower trays, the voices
          in your jerryd head

says nothing else for heroes, proof
says saves me when the words vibrate

     , says stop

a reminder for bruce

up to discreetly drawn & buried; older minute
worn of principles grand & grating
          , dresses like the room his wife
in orange walls & brown; *suggestiveness*
                    grown bloom of curved glass
, images are closer still; in stars & rags
& letters writing wrongs
                    here & here & here

a digital morph of utter names
& cancer, sliver; trick you walk, a trinket
eggs a boulder seed of trestle
          & a new construction; nameless
a drop-point, etched of vagueness
                    & desire-clamped

would you never you would die w/out

completed fancy, force of habit takes
you type forever; what would a barter boom
but in advance, emerge

          or myth a premise eastern heart
          to trinidad or mother mum

prepare to bead; prepare to ordinary stream

a valentine for melanie

the rules are supplied simultaneously; oh would you do
unruly live a line a short wide range
of weeding; band & empty bottles
the history of space
                              & complicated pines
a liquid now breaks down
, shot glass; working to digest wild boar or elk
would master of the shadow stoic hunt

                    in whose display? a foot in door & crowds
go pleasing by; she armrest thin
as *famous penultimate words,* look stoneward

little breath, the arms particularly cradled black

has left a drafting plane, a table
weed-goth makeup eye
                    she burns she burls she goes out

hardest against expressed degrees, these moments
regular the end of bar the pour
of endless

                    would a heaven of facts
                    in writhing landscape birds

of speaking prosody come kitchen-hence
a hesitation distance

a saint for jw

a maple mask, an envelope; a list of old stocks
rate lower than the combined freeze
              of self-defence; heartened rows
of socks *a thick oak found farewells*
would *piece me thus*, & undisclosed

                      what else is lag but just
a theory; log this; *say the name* & sainter
bicycle excursions
        ; absence is deliberate; a telephone
fair-well dusty tacks & each meant *paradoxical*

a journey-fed, in bucket-thin

approach the steps a *miracle bent in thirds*
& candour, sacred cup & filter

writing out a semblance to dissolve a sentence
etched in hand; *solution-ferry*

past is but a purple page of holes
& sainted listing left wing lean

& decade slide

       a flavour; having bit so much

a vowel for max

his umlaut invade; spring quickens
into a dead ironic
            would letters break in street
signs of supple measure, paint white sheet house
crescent makes; would you spring a thrill
            a building fourteen-storied
lemon throws, a lime; a hand that creeps up
out from blunder
                        nervous scores
a many subscribed now, or freezing axle grease

what up from turn; a minute
            I can tell you doors
a kitchen-spiel; a bottle snatch of wine
& poses; well-execute collusions
                        ; *naught made out of speech*

as time begats all audience, string
of theory winds a weather-mane
            to labours-lost
                        (*bring out your dread*)

I am begin again abstract

a hearse of many colours stole

a valentine for rhonda

what would not be believed; an oracle high
of horses perched an opposite ledge
                of night-tracks, noon a never-lended
, landscape thrill & blind a fire
                        ; *who target*, as they occur
a blandished mine of *rainfall*, standing

I uppermost a war-torn plain; the very edge
the world unfinished flat
        as every day, *a room w/ thousands, as it seems*

birds in the pool sin scrying, fingers
circle squares of well-wish, *pennies lopped*
& mornings an immutable glance

                the difference houses
, holds a latch-key principles, engagements
dresses drawers of fishers & red hair

would ark up bluntly; flies w/ money,
sugar-bees & sink house buckles,
warps beneath the weight

all around the saint john shadows
a mist of fists go hammer against cloud

a valentine for sean + kira

intuit a scene; a stranger longer sparks
, seraphim; hold the leg five hundred pounds
                    a man; an exit/entrance
out of every turn
                            , list a house from structure
tinker-toy complete, to mimic mercury & flower
drawn up from overlapping waves

                    save me, save; held offset
set in tears; together known as interest,
love, unmentionable
                            or what you would
slim pickings, trilo-bite a brain
or longer
                            not contains of love
but building blocks, self-replicate possessed

for feeling out a sentence; reroute tragedy
& riddled
                    being isnt everything; but see

a lane of low cost, man of so

to table-top an invitation; would
        a song of slew

& clarity of superstition; & a pulse
                    if only

a valentine for mari-lou

what broken travel, tortures; an insufficient pan,
or thirty-three consumption
                              : *type versus facts*
a stain not paper, horace-thick
entropic bait a science made of wasps
& disappearance
                                        handful saskatoons
& garden would you shovel-grow

a thousand tells a picture; *words may be read*
if I, attention then by contrasts
or a moral tension, jocular
                    a figurine the bamboo shoots
& leafy forecasts

a balance will the days; *vancouver-lost*

        rain hecks a white outside to amber,
gradual forget themselves; a searing fawn
of gradient to apples-thin

in kubla cant a rosary an ear

develops nicely; would razer-thin a breath
to molecule between

to overwhelm; & stagger subsequent divide

a song lyric for james

a balder tone of swim-tan, stroller
wednesday-blue a corner digger-deep constrains
           , *what riddled your chatter*

teeth isnt every blue or thirty-ness, thin
, a light-heeled warbling bass line, stare
the fries are off the sun

what limited-works in keys, translation
lateral the skin, a mortar bleed
of fictions, finally
                      lavender to being

do you remember when I told I wouldnt? there,
believe it; think-high colour scheme
of engines, catching breath
               in jam-jars punched w/ hurricanes

how rumours start; a magpie float
harmonica, foundation turn in hills
that airplanes spark
                        continuous or measure
letters screwdrive into sauce

& capo, chorus, capo; repeat as needled
, loop

a picture frame for danny

a causal-stop forgetfulness; numbed or numbered,
lettered on the spot
                        , *a lemon-painted scent*
of bodies & girls eyes; shining
would through a sense of order, shining fluke
& icy; assembling river-rail & blue
into tomorrow-jars

        a mindful marble is to spare
as what to carried, leaves shake blackness
quilt to blacker sky; *it always*
                happens somewhere; dogs
november howl, historied others
or a country barely dust & bone

        where nothing is for sale
& nothing wasted; politics means the skull,
& peace is just another country
                        , *tempra wash*
in egg & ipper, acid
south the base of brush

backfill through the canvas end of earth
too far along; would we back gasp

& invite the show of strollers park
& seesaw elemental coast

a valentine for karen

entropic; ten states instead of one; *a pharmaceutical*
                                        grace
        ; had missed beginning but she came on time
, any wonder, not being geographic, pocket stone
what happens in the sky; *did he*
            mention words

that angel/devil stare; a t-shirt shallow grey
& outside, all that you would mention
porcelain-thin; to irrational only forget
back into another, meeting side
                    & rattle back

cycles bring your short hair glossy grown from eyes

there are so many plastic episodes; vanishing thoughts
in bluenose pert a spiel
            coyote onion, oceanic trade
& back for nothing, chicken-wire

go two-by-two in twenty-one months

its faster than mother its faster than the painted bird

a pint for michael

trigger-toy, a formal archive truck
of lifted sense; fifty-odd passenger hours, unseen
training mummy drops; *is overgrown*
            & joyous; through retrospect in blue

a standard lowering deep-fry; seconds
by the pond
                ; would hear you breathe
from captured flags, a firearm
goes fishing crucible toward
                 ; *burn roman*
a royal hunch of oak impassive
multiple beauty tones
     would ring out wrinkling; *straightened out*
& softened; creates a weight in gold

gone tank to town a perfect pen example
, beneath the round

tune in to watching; archived cars
. & cuneiform displayed between a case

of salty depth
               ; could set
      your watch upon

a simple heartfelt twenty-minute hour

a valentine for wanda

wishing brush up on the east & *what*
lacks height; a muscled lore of branches
                        creation-thin; who knows
dramatic continent like you
                                , toss & turn
a backup constantly allowed for irish stage-breath,
blue in corners, curtain
                        down on all below

delay a layered nightmare voice a clock
                        whoever died

        ; a famine lung of leaving, boats come empty
, boats go; double-fan of elegiac jars

paternity of oxygen, & dead boughs
                        ; it was just as then to think

what do you get when you drain empty? what
                do bury ghostly in live earth?

; *if the knowing gets cracked*

        ; the world is falling water going up again
, of spades called aqua & marine

a near-miss for una + randy

another talk; write of whats known; limbs
   go buckling under; sweet tooth
& a celtic dream in fields of wake & grace

    to strike inherited skin & stare
, a moon goes glisten on guitar, a folk
of blue fools, black sheep shearing noon
& such familiar
     action is the only retreat,
where ships go passive, night
a think of shoes go strike on gravel waves
& what else river meets
  & practiced tunes
     a book on tape
in colour schemes & cycling

   a warm clump resting shore on shore
   an airplane level blackberry thin
    & stretching hours

what else from the golden time of heaven, riddled us annoy?

what else time an idea truly is but blush?

a valentine for suki + elaina

a neighbourhood wash; constructing pint of blue
& unforgiven; turns the tables off
    , limited-use of polished stock, particularly
of prose & envy; a basement room recording waves
& smell, an occupation

                heat behind a distance

correction to the sunlight, parties gone
& mornings up, unasleep a passenger rise
          of pleasing measures, dancing girls
& drag queens

         ; *into a spruce frustration*
a comets breath of heaven, held
        & quartered

lights are lifted, left & paths
       , in symmetry
           takes you
bridging body & body, hope & combined hope

; *the rules*
     go ticket under; multiple,

              & some

am down & structure into moments optimism pulled
the very centre; a game of random suspect never

an invitation for david + dorothy

to assuage a local; dinner-sense
instead of drink
                        are lost & moulded small
a spoon or kitchen runs askew

        ; rhymes w/ muses, blue cloth cylinder
a garden function, important points
of floating beasts, like children, imagined
                in generic possibility

                        ; *how envelope a poses*
walks elgin street a broad stem volume
soaks up clouded hands & stones
, or ripples up the rideau

        bridge is but a berryman, an utter jump
of singles left behind
                it was like being
underground or such, translating language taught
korean circles wide & widened
                ; a library, such a delicate shore
                                of numbers

fashion a burn of winter honey, prague turns
bent into a picture

        (*what hasnt happened yet*)

a first sip glows a pyre multiplies

a question for my mother

what do my echoes mark; too much for one plus one
plus something other; immanent & spring,
                    controlling change of break-wit
, slipper sharper tongue
                              the horizon followed me home

            ; would show up in each others dreams
of celtic wash & dreadnaught, an english white
no other hue will stick to
                    ; *is never easy*; a body made of mud
& bone construction, guilt a while
sense indignant waves & unforgiveness

            a week of seeking possibilities in streets
                         that buckle under; holes
            that once they knew you, filled

        as green wood grew around

                    ; your kitchen-blue was yellow,
metaphor, a prose of chairs I painted scrape
bare down to roots, the tree
            ; an edge you barely fashion, knew

if versions compare themselves to radiator, hill
& stumbling resistance

                              ; teethmarks

a logoryph for roland

if never-ending; perch a craft on picket fences
burnished, worn immediate
    a wind withdrawn in mute
        a thousand would emit

in staple-cars astrological & large
    as any coastal wonder; *beware of meteors*
& icebergs, both; slink or journal swim
, a crowd against the heat
        of crossword stars
    & paint-by-number clouds

a lateral miracle would by any other be a name

starker-teen & late transmission, gods
made out of clay; *the plum trees*
    slipped stalk of nature
, spurned or cheated
      every question
has its root in numbers

retreat a step an ever widening winter arc

a valentine for anne

quarterslip missing; a poster streetsville dream
of field & pilfered fence; *you cant*
                    grow home again
; the rest of body either, wither
                              but a joke
          ; were perpendicular, fused
, a friday costume wasted

                                        doors a tudor front,
& hastings drains; what would go out through
& under
              ; *there is too much to want*

too much to keep track, too much
to remember to forget
                          or do you
, forward glasses long & blue-mule keefer light
& parties on
                    & what a pear tree
                                        used to
you cant blow home; or sewn up quick
the hem of what you used to

              ; would keep a close watch eye
              & write a chill air even dawn

& what the stars were, going on outside

a manuscript for steve + cathy

if through the cowgirl heat; a bottom, enters
mid-summers sunday & a best
                    of countless-dog nights
; *would closer you would be at house*
                            , the legend of a sleeping king
        beneath a salisbury stake, a hill
that rolls horizon fore

            ; *the older paper get the more*

where entry, in a wealth of breath
volcanoes around, street realm of queens
                & glue pot, swizzles
, floor to floor to basement
                    , *never ground*

would goggles prose a beauty lent constrains
all versions
                    ; methodical & thus
a twin-bear warm

        to where a sleep & lack of sense

an ending, thus; made real today of short quick work

a valentine for kathy

to intro thinking; the bar or even draft
would strike a dumb or drum, *an image curls*
                discursive skin;
to keep your things; a heartfelt must,
                      inherited blocks of gold
        & silver ruin; *a mordant*

if does become a preference; a last gauge sky
undercutting trace-lines; vague anxiety
           of tones & tunes & crescents
, *would utterance, a phone call measure*

                              ; coffee lightly, burn
or hustle buses
            ; would that eternity is, restraint
a jar of kitchen-blue, a tarp
            of gardens concrete creep

       & never salvage; *against neither nor*
or suffering, sin

         ; a breaking tonal shift of furies
                made of chocolate, bees

& even only denser reference is clean

a caution for david

go causal & think; breathe out a three-hole
                 blasted; fish-hooked mouth, the bottom
of an endless bay
                 ; *look homeward, strangle*
metaphysical & deeper bait
       you weapon would be out; go
                 eaten alive

a tire pulls it, toilets, sink already sold
           for two-hand glue; *a painted face*
of poets in a backyard dream, the basement
studio lawn
                 ; from the outside wait, the children
dressed up to fill
       our rural origins

we knew the leaves of shells & slaving propaganda

           ; muses worn for sleeping
& the plague, a rid disease yawns tenderly
, curse unfurled of *each house*
           you stepped into

time a drift; electrode cross
         the border south

go safer in; they never will forgive

a postcard for suzannah

a buckled praise; if orbit horribly in charge
or split decision;
                              hard moulded to a word
a swiss to safety, archive alps
& family to swim w/; soccer plays,
                    but passive interest seen
; black clouds concentrated against snow

                              nothing smaller burns,
dark watching changed, as in a foreign dream
of cars & jars, canadian winters
            & an africa built of beads & worry
; *where are you now*
                    ; the writing of this wisdom pearls

a pumice stone, brief history
of neglect, a country pandemic through
            a trembling cup, an open grill

would corresponding mark in january, july
would to any of various larger kinds
                    of english, broken
        if at all

giving out a kind of story a culture painting sticks
an active copy; *rivers made of gold*
            excuses, castor sugar blackened

& a tourist milled
for when you finally home

a prop for chuck

made curiosity, seeming child; jill waits,
patient & forever always
                        ; a missing thirteenth passion-page
; *would through his scratch & morbid*
                                ambivalence; a smartest made
; curious to touch, a look or look upon

            , on ragged river steps, breaking all news
placed in jars, or northern burn so natural
you couldnt wait to leave;
                        get up
from the children woke, a kitchen chair
when let before; *we talk*
        we love, we find ourselves

a history of the colour blue vancouver waves & blood

this bottle followed me home, & heart
the voice from here
                        scraped out
            what I decided; square rochester light

if trick & lime you, sear us pass
the wall moves quietly, magnum flask

        what baby gesture finally happens
        neither from towards or too

& then make three; hair falling over eyes

a valentine for marianna

if youth is blunder, benefit; w/out having moved
flows into, under
      ; cavalcade of downhill further sky
would reach in language swell & deep
translating grief & wonder, complaints
      a lighthouse, every day

or writing slip around a blink; you regular,
cool evening in the dark or backyard,
      mothers ilk, a blue & blue-screen
five foot angel mute
& grown unknown, foot under hem
        mysterious; *or ever was*

thousands, it seems; we thought so, prohibitive
an evening sky of heat
      & uppermost; a war-torn
length; would replica a greek piece
held on either side

an hour stretch, a big screen mess of days & undelivered

why do you ruthless the divide & watered?
why do the weather plastic
      reassures the peninsula skin?

why else do you crack & curl a laugh
      synonymous booming,
    fires at the top of your throat would melt

at exactly the same time?

a compass for gil

betwixt a prose of awful curiosities w/out limit,
antagonism waits
             & sorrows, east coast
north a flower draining, drawing blue
; collect unmentionables, in tongues & jars
         a beauty riddled into being
, never seen
           & envied for a time

; *sleep calls attention,* what else held you would
(*turn left, here*) murmurs nerves a blend
         of fourteen colour schemes
& bled; man-made divisions
        heart & soul
; what keeping yours, a volume
      predicates & safety, burnished burns

what all the film crashing, frames

what waterlogged or is, retired from vault
& mirror-held
         I watch for cars

all sentence for a reason; prose for fact
& colour stripped

     a fact in world in different banks

there can never violence be enough, in tooth

a window-shade for brendan

an artichoke heart; twin is as does,
what nonsense withers; *insect hopes*
        & civilization noise
a cottage campers starts w/ prizes
all who ever died
            or did; what even
clocks stop, chimneys still remain
a children door to door a crescent

         ; a pendulum turns a wheel
a key would find a lock, whip bees the back of hail
& sifting rafters, warm air gathers thick
           in mason jars
; what old grandmothers make; standing music,
they clutch each narrative touch
      where aperture appears, a closet
          groping homemade wine
             & curls

kitchen is where everything the blade the knife is living
sixteen family arms
        & keeping

translate schools & all else two by strangle two
the shape of movements tall the grass

    you lawn she lawns they all lawn

sugar still a girl, a name
        a spice so double sweet

it burns

a deflection for ken

the borders in a bad mood; or hopeful grown
of maine house missions, local beers
; the dawn that shot the dusk
                              , four towns over

english into makes one someone; following a flavour
trestle-track, a new-type terrors
                    ; there are lines left opening a drawer
of little gaps, gasps; one day is blind
; what one box represents

          ; *what would you do but utter names*
; if books would some at vernal speeds
& variety, pushed; he bows respectfully,
he hinders tree
                    in gesture silence
          ; *mirror-word, goes greatly*

travel constant & alone; the sea south warbles
bird song so much older, than
                    ; *a key is blowing solitude,*

a lock is holding door; would temporal qualities
printed volumes you would matter
          & contend
                    stroller-deep a blue

; *a whistle blows; you younger & you grab a rein*
of shifting, now

a valentine for angela

would speech that never-saves; decomposition blue,
or natty-chatter through the weary *hands*
                 kept clear of unseen vision, polished particulars
; *had felt like long ago*, the golden sand
of summer, a fling down highway

                       , gravelled gracefully under
up to my needs in knees; a coastal pattern
drives & bridges, shoots & leaves, *at least I know*
                  how lovely
; alphabetics of shift-work, slaving periodics
one into one makes; what were you, sleight of hand

a laughter peeled from last lights, torn string at the regular

        ; the worlds longest hope doesnt start or show
no knowledge, noise & necessary

when you were, so obligations, dream
& dream-blood; what was knowing but a heavy case
               of what

through sugar discreetly rises, slabs an outstretched hand

the words hum here & garland, nuptual
wear thin breakfast

& make their way past eyes

July 20-31, 2006
Ottawa ON

open (prose) body: twenty-one (incomplete) poems

(for Lea Graham)

the body incontrovertible. does not lie.
    — Daphne Marlatt, "Out of the Blue"

skin is kin
    — Karen Hofmann, *Water Strider*

the language does not die young
    — Garry Gottfriedson, "Koyoti Indian"

neck

stills into an inconvenient nightmare.
construction comes in jars. the only way to
leave this place is to deliberately lift.

everything is gentrified. the peel of a taste
of skin over blue sky blue is a layer of dust.
the skin that would otherwise be.

I am hopelessly incomplete; I am hopeless
and this. green car passes, shakes; green car
is the key to a pardon.

today I am human; thrum on its neck.

recall

in the first place there is someone currently
occupied. is this the next time or the last?
the car is never where left.

impossible through the bushes, impossible
one biggest caterpills. crawls through, lets
the layers, low.

do you know anything about yellow the
helmets in snow.

when I loved I completely but now cant
recall.

still

situational, room is only room. perhaps
this is only the best. perhaps this noise the
furthest from truth.

if in fact there is noise.

this corner of somerset harbours holes in
the ground, a small plastic duck. the water
remembers the shape of the stone.

if a crushed language leaps. if chalk rolls
through the window or still.

behind

a poem writing largely hopeless where you
broke out the bough. I couldn't address.

formality from other towns would overlap
these concerns. it would only threaten
theatre. the senseless begin.

with one hand you slow.

do you remember the question; or jimmy
hoys place? the dust in the mouth more
than dry.

would you leave (accidental) behind.

grotesque

some morning coiled subway in stations,
the way of empty promise. rideau street
makes aware the routes of proximity.

three wrongs make it; pencil-thin and red
dragons awake, the night halloween
forgets, stops being a question.

are you getting this? are you backbiting
unrehearsed beauty?

a terrible mode of grotesque.

enter

the most important flirt on the wagon;
hold on, its nothing. the taxi cabs breeze
through the aisles.

were you brick in the little house.

were fundamentally unclear, to be system
or present a belief still means nothing. and
bestow this, what reason.

am I city lights or you?

a season you interdrift, a right you would
enter.

truth

a neighbourhood begins where it ends, in
the body. all critics reside there.

I am hollow, all subsidy.

high tech balloon to the furthering west
where the city bends boundless. the city
bounds. an eastern pall burns.

would you trouble or heart-rend.

what we practice to turn; sandy beatings,
where everything sets. would loom large a
disturbance.

men at work carwash; the likeliest truth.

smokes

stride confident, calmly through maps and
be spectacle. bespectacled.

I am rumi; removed.

would sit there and static; or a record of
flax on a seahorse; the sink and the swim?

is interesting uncle, pull back or the arm.

the room smokes from within. smokes.

moss

this winter wanes trace in my summer skin;
tune in to chill, or go warmly in view. is
inflicted a car.

lot metre and gravel; wheels tire, catch
stone into waver. drive into bone.

release, catch; go at all the wrong orders.

back the highway commercial. write top-
down to heaven in blank damp moss.

living

or plenty mistaken. from a series of works
go through lightly. eighty percent.

subvert written to greasy.

concretely the mind curves in imperfect
english; meant screwed for a while. in
humour, or some circumspect.

a commodity style of time hollow trees.

I am unhappy so wither; does this bridge
beam a living?

refrain

a composer, through means independent.
was wondering slim. was a theme through
a bend soccer maimed?

horticult. splice virtual divide or canal.
more spiders and woe down the wall. says,
brush often.

let poker refract; painted window refrain.

thing

would through from a savagery. blue
connecticut words. is this known as letting?

one read from his lips a soft willow with
bees. the lawn longs for criticism.

building bodies of hair and of stone.

is this large despite rejuvenation? is this
detail despite the one smallest thing?

spend

would know you from still incomplete.
dont worry, you things; a world shifted
noun for the drudgery.

a battery-operated mime. would you think
out a wonder of graceless pages and torn,
deflowered trains in the postbox.

all you could do would be fill it.

out bendable mess; three wheels are fastest
to turn. to afford all your time out to
spend.

hold

misplaced depends. wheelbarrows
announce georgian flood and the damp.

receiver burn would you.

interject tasteless and worn; the rain skin
buckles under. a knapsack she twirls
careless on tables and floors.

an example of politics speculate.

tomorrow would (possible) thunder storms
hold.

birthday

where theory is bull; compassion, a
backdrop of gangs. a lattice in cables.

first awesome swings; you glasses. a
testament as clear and as carved-out as
joyce.

if you wistfully manage.

an ottawa twirl of the writ; at pubwells we
window know. we ask for a birthday.

tension

almost a grown-up; on particular days
makes no scientific sense.

a pampered fallow.

to skeleton fore; out a pilgrim of cars or of
needles, time stretches a digit.

or low soil milled; mine a tunnel out.

cross one with blindfolding, a neat
desktop. feet scribe concentrics, tension.

from

call jack spicer demons. demonicus. a rage
against spruce street the corner barn.

an idea of their balcony, swings.

no present like time; would work names in
the undercarriage. oft couples chain paper,
claim currents.

the many questions of spicer. a space and
significant from.

his

at the end of the street, a bar; two men
walk into it. a burn sun-drowsed.

was looking in back, at a suburb.

how do you convince out a city? come the
new year, a plane catch on cushions and
strings, a sombrero a minute to mention. it
swings.

particular, years. couple realized in brush;
death count.

except for collecting his.

cold

all overcoat, gloves; the shape of a centre-
filled. intangibilities, adrift, rubber lips.

would she simply dream still?

she would forget one defended. scuttling
truth, flavours out of a rut. gone traditional
scant.

a resonant lyric, burst.

dear darkness, I begin that I think growing
cold.

field

little fish, I swagger solitudes at face,
burning bridges. why do you centuries
meeting plow, stake. men without hats
pasture.

I want you to want you.

little returned home, the sleep trouble
classics, a history margins me.

of cynical hards; heart-harded.

email suggestions, the goal is to find bitter.
a field.

beside

this language lifts, the technical 'out of the
world' embits, embibes knowable. three-
pronged submit.

oh lord would you.

forever anon, all too human a microscope.
peer sixty-seven. she wages my age as she
ends, well.

if the french, he suggests, just have deeper
thoughts down. a sound immune then to
ages.

or figuring wand; a dancer the point,
beside.

weightless

(for Jordan Scott & Juliana Spahr)

A city is always a lost city.
— Lisa Robertson, *Rousseau's Boat*

This is how the story goes:

A peacock became a man
and soon enough fell in love
with a woman.
— Shannon Bramer, *The Refrigerator Memory*

I was not in love, so I was free.
— Kristjana Gunnars, *The Rose Garden*

We come into the world.

We come into the world and there it is.
—Juliana Spahr, *Gentle Now, Don't Add to Heartache*

*

under shadow & shawl. alive but for the wrong moment, underground. weightless, formless, knowing nothing but what is underneath. all that is all & nothing is above you now.

I am looking out the window at crocuses. they no longer know their colour. winter is coming. does it feel like I am only half paying attention? does this lack of attention bother you?

*

I know nothing abt the name or colour of the rose.

the wind a damp whistle; the kind of bark it chews
regards striations naming age. where would
we follow.

you said you would not embarrass me, ever.

would I wantonly call you anything; a name
that I would call you, any.

the fire a standard; the corner of somerset
& spadina, eleven pm. we know now winter comes.

she is too far gone to be burnt out; she is too
far gone.

I remember a feeling of weightlessness.

I remember an image.

*

Gertrude Stein wrote, a rose is a rose is a rose is a rose. its not
the flower but the language we seek. the name
at the naming core.

if we could nip this in the bud. I mean, would we?

I am willful telephone; I am willful days & nights. I am
Carnegie, the last man standing.

at the end of our senses I am waiting. if I
am pressed for meaning.

means overruns me, outweighs. a meaning. he thinks it is this way in this
way in this. is this. this pearl of wisdom. what?

strange & delusional, I am marking my territory w/ weeds &
w/ thistles. do you remember that summer we spent? or by the
house in Toronto the owner decorated w/ toys & bells & whistles
& figurines. like living in Susan Musgrave's car.

I have not been able to find it since. your red red scarf. the tang
of your fresh grapefruit sweet.

[~~I am neither passive nor pigment.~~]

*

a sweater brings weather, a winter brings warmth
a slew out from any, if there is utterance, weight

wait for it, weight; ambivalence & trees; we would
later; [a ~~quarter pounder~~]

I didnt recognize you w/ yr curly hair
[~~as we all have curly~~

~~somewhere~~]; weightless bleed; through weightless days
& nights I wonder, the largest dark

if you sling below shore; I am body-logged,
water floating deliriously on water

& under; surface rots of a tension below
one base, & what element

is denser than two; are you ever?

thanksgiving monday the second cup
no newspapers; leave all the locals

staring into space not newsprint

*

hegemony is everywhere. I am
far off light between her strength.

a moment exclaims one. in the elevator,
going down

we were weightless for a moment, moment.
by the moonlight, brushing canadian flag

outside the albert & bay suites. where
were you yesterday? if I call you

will your husband know? what

is all this knowing?

*

inside,
        I am filled w/ problems,
your problems, of which I am

but one.   the hearts knowing glare,
defied, denied, a drink is this
desirous of forms

& deliriums, deadly. a black widow
that lets everyone live.

alive on cloud, spoiling; drifted
down the hill to lebreton flats.

what is a memory [but empty fizz,
once the soda goes flat]? what are

these energies in reserve, preparing
to reverse?

[I have already paid the price.]

*

I am sick of ease. collectively, I make
a statement concerning bowler hats

& the fall divine, shadowed in light.

this is hardly the end of things. days,
nights. by now a strand a daughter,

shot the whole thing through gauze,
in 8mm. the seat of fame tickles.

the not tourists on the soil but dressed
in the fine clothes, breaking

from delayed pullings. the far west
& the far east wondering.

company of divine & the sun.

soil plants out density & fuels begin.

*

a hopscotch heroes jane; how dare she flaunt?
like wings of angels; young demons pull

like children, flies, except
it forms a human. a merely obsessive

through horizons & the plate, 22 km
in any direction

before the earth curves. subtle, she says,
the din. I am up against trees & redwood,

& the last time you recommended anyone.
slight & beautiful, she says, & married

once before. who hasnt been?
I said.

or my finger, where I pulled
my strays.

*

[~~through days & sleepless~~] an ache
that pains me. desirous of forms [

] awake, dear twisted. the sheets
are still [a mess]

warning factions of pastoral, geopoetry
[~~the myth of sameness & preservation~~]

a man turns back time to live w/ bears
& gets eaten alive; records

[~~his own screams & empty ribcage~~]

where once his humours, heart; collected
bile that kept [~~victorian glance~~]

does a cameraman [~~shit in the woods?~~]

can a wild animal do anything else
at the smell [~~of blood?~~]

[~~I am so much sleeping time~~]

*

to say, I do not even know the name.

discolourization is not the same thing (after
countless rehearsals).

the matter of one part betrayed, the
matter of phrase, duration.

a very slips itself in blindly

are you looking at me?

in my mind, the piano a dead instrument
[~~oh, to be surrounded by it~~].

*

new cable on my old bicycle, half-cut.
I am living on borrowed [bicycle] time.

the empty space under curry, *it must
be rice*, from soulful bookstore w/out soul

to a driving school w/out parking. the space
between moments.

the day inflates & the sun rises, breakfast
& bad coffee, I remember speech.

I remember speaking. she was lovely,
wasnt she.

out of sandy hill for the right now.
staying out of harms way.

*

to be, she says, to be   in bee space, yellow
beeswax black, through pigments
entered luminous deep

a labyrinth of thin sound
floor & feather, norwegian faces

to feel, hear, taste, touch & question

to be, she says, she only says
drugstore horoscope scrolls all numbered, up
to thirty-one
                    a nordic trace

to create an earthquake; awake inside
an eruption of bees

eruption of canvas marking older, other

                    (for val roos

*

what is happening between blades of grass
what is weightless

what is observed from window ledge from window
sill from doorway from the forest floor
what is weightless

what is harbouring a mean streak
what is weightless

what is deafness falling ears
what is weightless

in the clocktower pub she when handed a pint
what is weightless

long through the cultural emnity; through fire
what is weightless

I am long in through another
what is weightless

I am bewildered; scream
what is weightless

the edge of an edge of another edge which is probably
in the end a line
what is weightless

wonder at photographs on walls; the bottle
on reflected shelf her glasses wake
what is weightless

his head shaved grey to white to clear like tiny straws
what is weightless

[gentle now, I fiction]

*

faithless; stateless

a month into an ampersand; first snow,
tire stripes & slush   a truck hits kitchen
muscle shirt, *daredevil*

a predicament of bees, & genetic
purpling
                    in several scenes
obligate, heretofore

[crept into the text]; relinquish,
if never for

heart out a heartstill

sunlight; islands & breathes

*

accumulation,
                    if you are a gesture,
accumulate; a strand of whiter hollow hair
form the exclamation, point

a conifer, confers; stream out, [he called
his daughter] colour if there were some

blue, & a red, & a blue

undeveloped, the frame goes weak

*

how it scars on skin   painful icons,
an admiration mark

if breathing is a breath away; away

paper so hard against the sentence; a sentence
of faithless years & flames

says serenity; says surrender

I am notebooks; in spite of grading, gradient
& rapid fire through sleep

is anyone even; listening?

the fourth wall; down & down to enjoy
the root of a snake

a prairie shack; a memory of eighteen

*

enemy or nemesis
                    the words are not used
deliberately; long lines & limpid

find, where she was   coupling,
arteries appear in the world

& abandoned sock, the foot of the bed
(not so good w/ people)

did you room w/ a bunch or a folktale,
a line limps flat & a line

evolves; absolves

ashen; [the bagless cat]

*

a (weightless) memory of normal

if fear is a state, or a still-line province
                        ; the district of, amorphous
                        & slow
                        slow

begets a terrible beauty

means nothing a speak speech

clearing; a sworn statement warm in the hand
; hearth, harken

a manifesto deep in the tongue

(extra hot hot heat) delineate,
obscure

I remember everything abt tenure
& being born

when rock is a rock until man makes
stone
                        , a tool

*

I have never done; harpsichord
chordless
, walks around the house a
good long time

bicycle sits out; slaughter a lark land

thins out slightly; sly; a maverick pose

if body begins to lose; lonely alone
is no different than lonely
[w/ someone else]

thin stream of streams; veins collapse
chalk river, erodes; erodes like dust

& settles, unsettling
a powder down a trace; if I cam
hateful : hollow

intrinsic a summer walking path from house
to house to yard

, hole in fences, tense

107

*

slow hand marbles (weightless) floors & floors are
; baited, breath
        of casual shadow; causal

a manual of how they looked when they looked
how they touched   the bare cells
                        of their hands

waving weightless & warm; shallow

ere an air; brenouli; thread a thin wind
there & through there

                        bears repeating
                        bares, repeating

know it is & then is;   (jeanne) d'arc
                        & (gilles) de rais

        darkened array

like a moth to her; like a sloth
to a flame

ash flicker french; air

*

lemon eyes; jersey smile
let slip a bridge

a beginning; begat,

      cornered   three sides
                                of still

honorific; pair came down on the ice

is this hockey or is this something else?
something other?

              mars   :   the planet
                                    & chocolate bar

                                    closer than they have been
                                    together

                                    n years

staring out a stable

                 (for sina queyras

*

newspaper asks　　　:　　　who are you listing to?

whats in the bag

　　　　　　a lens as long
　　　　　　as your long circle arms

unavailable by email or phone

stately; stated merely as fact; if a trouble
　　　　　　　　　　is troubled enough

　　　　　　　　　　　　mis-align;　　in

　　　　　　　　　　　　　　　　co

　　　　　　　　　　　　　　　　here

*

w/ the first stone, weightless in the hand
worth two in the bush

                                , synonymous
            hand-held,

                        the sudden myth of tulips
                        in the window by the desk

where did they come from? whom?
external to this, an email

            from her work I am not allowed;

is this where you think; this

                                the feet & the back of her hands

an underside   :   which way
                                    is which

            [purple springs & rain,
                    if gear in the knot]

a shift, heart of intuition; & surrounding words

*

what stars are up   pushing
                                 down

the particular angle of the body
the particular angle of three sides
                          against

            of apollo twelve, the apple
            strikes the weight waiting noggin

a signal goes forever in space
w/out a body to block it

            or receive

                          if you were even there
                          ; mark zero three dot nine

in the photography you can hear

*

to realize (still) I am this; manmade

                 scrapes from the sky behind; a colour
                 orange, blue
                 on the rocks

        behind the city centre

a tree is black empty space another CCCA building
is black & blackened trees

                 I know when I (thot I)
                 loved her then
                 I know that I haven't
                 anymore, dont

               in a long time

      "you think you understand
      how really broke (n) I am"

I am tired of telling you this [

             ] I am empty, degrees
I am waiting, degrees
I am waiting, weightless, degrees

        a million miles of dust
        metric, metric, I am
                 imperial still

            your hesitation holds me here
            beside mine

wave arms in protest; perfect

*

it begins w/ the end
the end is departure

trace my days through coffee cups

the pulse of isolating phrases; get back
classic; the sun goes down

jerry drives his green car ½ a block

brockwell through the air; sends poems
from blackberry

black
berries

transit is intransigent; is only reasonable
& clear

is nothing (else)

[~~sex at thirty-eight~~] unfinished shield notes: letters to g.

*

The skin thin parchment.

Its word, the
word for it, whispered here.
　　— Erin Mouré

I can no longer keep a journal. My life erases everything I
write.
　　— Robert Kroetsch

This is not about music this is about desire. The desire that rides us,
four horses on a carousel. When the music stops we are obligated to
change horses. How did I, the first violin, learn of desire this
temperate man this musician of controlled vibrato and perfectly
creased trousers? There was a spot on her hand and it preoccupied
her immensely. She rubbed at it, a cat with buttered paws.
　　— Méira Cook

Geography is not the point here, it's the landscape we make
on the page [...].
　　— Lee Ann Brown, *West Coast LINE*

continued shield notes:

the bone across the soft flesh
is only bone

a completeness of virtues spread
from tree to distressed tree, compressed

into a boundary of north

what is the impulse of barriers
& transformation

into violated frontiers? what would
your father

think of me? the chinese wall
of ontario, shield

an endless, sudden relief

rice lake: how could any cold lake
in such a province

otherwise be filled

[~~sex at thirty-eight:~~] a discovery poem

realizing there is nothing left to discover
but for everything else

we had never occurred, the map of my mouth
opening up

your west. I am writing you now
in discovery; just as you

would write me. like columbus or cook,
learning what someone else already knew,

but never knew. this is the arrogance
of the foreigner. learning too late

the difference

between understand
& overtake. so how I long

to understand. small endless fires
distant.

help please me to know.

[~~sex at thirty-eight:~~] a list

this is the body
this is the book
this is a list of where you have entered
       & have entered me
this is the subject
this is your leg over my leg
these are your blue blue eyes
this is a citizen walking aimless
       through course
this is the first time
this is the last
this is a letter hammered into stone
this is the body, not symbols
this is the sweat under snow
this is the body working past lyric
       into post-lyric
this is the between rhythm, singing

on the canadian shield

I love you rock, my corner-stone
I love you littered w/ children
       & snow
I love you river, acrid
       on stony plain
I love you 19th century digression
       into the principle
I love you story, & its alternate
I love you, caught
       between trees
I love you myth, & the place
       of your myth-making
I love your distance, but I
       would rather
I love your history, & embrace
       at this joining; this entering into
I love what your future
       will consider this

love is a road
       we can only get by train

continued shield notes:

in space of human boundaries & geography,
so too, the space of five foot eight

blonde hair settles; I would write
"shimmering" (I would

remember you)

post-colonial slippage; a sweet
& little dimple when she smiles

an effort
that may sound slight

more lines to cross
than this one

across the boundary of evening, & one
less car to travel; out here, certainty
& love is everything

expanding out a certainty
into discovery

& discovered; a land no light could master

presuming, mister livingstone, a heart
of darkened light

[~~sex at thirty-eight~~] (lost in the barrens)

writing sex at thirty-eight a flight
of marking through the barren

patchwork black rock stubble
entreating wilderness of some

of pudding stone, a ragged fainting strand
made whole

of twoness, twosome; blood bold
into purple shadow scenes

we could have passed an isolated world

I read you tearing, stubble
three hundred miles south

a particle of belief; a catalogue
of longing, thirty-eight

& forty-one; we are as old
as centuries of trees; we are the newborn,

where even the familiar new,
& unforeseen

one fainting strand

I want to write you in as endless, a tour
but theres no one in it, write you in

to the continued story; the authentic measure
of the longest road

heart is made of muscle, heart; writing
made of language, lines

in my glittering dreams

at the end of dragonhearted sheer, the tavern
parkdale market long, I watched you leave

for hours more than you left me

a habit of crows & thorn depend; is there
the red wheelbarrow, market thrush

I want to write you in

I want to write around what else you
signed yourself, away

blank-blind & open faith

the practice of outside

would shade me a determined breath
would slide

would catch as catch
would make visible the air
would caution snow

would mark a magpie song
would substantiate a repetition

would hero at the fore
would court remembered meaning
would break up a begin

would shoreless inexhaustible
would weather storms
would, w/ every experience together

would at home differences
would genuine poetic depths
would strata, sub & sub

would drum beat lyrical rebirths
would love loving, reject rejection

would long against the wall
would occupy

continued shield notes:

this is a portrait against portraiture; a moment
parcelled into being

oh lord, let us be married all over ontario

a love of years & solitudes, the space
where rivers meet, the ottawa (grand)

& ste laurence, lake
of two mountains

a devotion to speed & shine, the bawdy
aspirations of birds & bees, an arrival

planet we would reach

not like swords in the path; a sea
of birch trees, flogged w/ lines

along a primal shore

I am enveloping a frontier beside you; I am
continually reimagining white space

& delicate strength, this knowing craft
into the wildwood

it writes: your love a series of endless lake

writing, unfinished g.

my unfinished helena, writing out
of bare-bone elements; finished craft
to launch a thousand circles
north to south; what is this distance
I have seen before, what has
grown longer & more wide
w/ each shortened step; I wonder,
time compressed, the vacuum ground
become immortalized, black blackened smoke
across the stone faced stone, I checked
the sequence of provide & watched
the forms diminish; where are you now,
where are you, I am wanting &
then wishing just where are you
& my ancient breath, a footfall
starved to catch up, could I then
have ever held, or held on, this is
elongated grief, delinquent
broken cup & desperate plea that would
fall silent, bent & bent upon

your borders are unthinkable

& silent
& supplemental lines

but west slope facing east

& would calamity the best guess
& wondering sex at any age, be it
    thirty-eight or where we

but came upon, a sense of dereliction
    & of duty

& work w/ what, discarded love
    that we would willingly take
& through an endless prayer I sit
    your naked feet

but prone would make me
    stone

& if betrayed face pleasure made to dream
    an end to all your heartache
& faithless I were not completed

but in a poem, lonely
    as a single vowel

& made out to be numerous
& made to coat your honeyed voice
    w/ actual

but to measure mine is insufficient

& would agreed upon, all love
& would work to risk all love
    & unattainable

[~~sex at thirty-eight~~]

expansive poem,
expansive love

body, then
no body

drizzle, then
a sharpness

pull of strings, a
heart-knot

letters to
unfinished, or
the letters

done themselves

unfinished, or
unsent

I write you out
& out then,
writing

[~~sex at thirty-eight~~]
& what else

glistens

expansion

unaccustomed to this present
limbs go weak, are unaffected

what madness, drives
to hotwire the past

a slovenly make; as adults, pretend
to know the difference

between real love
& imitated, pantomime

festooned; the breeze
cant hold

or what the difference sex
and endless love, two corners

of the wooden brush

& what depends upon
& what red wheelbarrow then scrapes

continued shield notes:

as papers papered
& collected in the field
& written bound, distilled
an entry made in waves

do not pass go

every morning he would wake
& make tea, collect
his notebooks
& record what he had seen

look, she said
look

the birds cry caw caw
cawcawcawcawcawcaw

the birds cry can
that can

unruly sex, the power
to bend spoons

backwards, not enough;
[at thirty-eight,]

to turn that spoon
to powder

sure as if by flowers

create this was were was none
loose a sure idealism

strong, a sex
would get sex, given

a fine grammar, set loose
on blood-bone

this invitation
cues a complex visual

given voice
to address the right hand, right hand
reaching

silences stored in memory

silences adrift, gone out
& stamen-fed

this bed of pollen; [~~thirty-eight
at sex~~]

against our primary tools

against this gesture of invented
possibility

a telephone, a letter

& a painful click; depends upon,
a narrative understanding beauty

you, & therefore you

would tongue an instrument; travel
headlong into framing; *where*

are you; confident that I will not wander,
venture into clouds

& then be lost again

amid a constant static; *what is my name,*
this measured bliss I will not

steward or secure;

a path of waiting; scored the corner
list of missing days

if this is love; strips naked & allows
as slippage, never

on the platform, word
& word she whispers in the ear

of what comes after

constellation

*

a method taped to the door. a burgundy curtain. the expansion of trees; collar smoke from the factory. sudbury squalls. the water indigent; the water indifferent, dying.

*

a long paper wonders; stomach lining. philosophy profs, props headframes. what holds the open door. I would recognize you, even the ring of your folder. this is a postcard from mars. I hold the moss in high regard. do you think of the weeds.

*

stars bustle & send. will articulate here. common practice, & a new relation. I am bendable, elbows & knees. a hearty telegram stock. would you process & please. I am bustle & blend; so lost.

*

a small engine whirls; rent temperature. said thank you; land lines separated by equal indistances. the space occupied by space. a wisp in a stare. an installation in figures. field failing a courtyard. there was never a court.

*

stand up and be mounted. young western duds in custom. I would delicious rain. you the time of her life. absurd living of while; pretend clouds. hunger the beauty myth, hunger the ears. I would change lovers to everything; an eye after looks.

sweat

thumbs down
from the blue

sex at a number
defies, defines

would entry a whole,
would subsequent set

a sweat, soldiered
on

one wants the connection
to remain

depleting chill, de
scends

& demarcation

if would soldier on

if would de
ep

end

[~~sex at thirty-eight:~~] canadian shield

to propose myself in order to propose
I write *my self*

a letter unfinished I include to you
to be included

so that

how can any draw a parallel
a step against a foot

or human conquest; *am I
not moving*

to include a reference point
to truly know

if stars once moved, the earth
stood still

come shooting stare

a constellation we would empty
& propose

in lieu of nothing

continued shield notes:

a boiled scar of (blended) sun

on the way up to the sound, we looked
& listened; *paused,* a bit

a commensurate action
, soundless rapture

a buildup, twenty years or more
of minor fumblings

where are you now; a judgment singular
& secure

how do you hold an absence

how do you hold a rebellion
in the troubled heart

once started, it cant
just begin

be done

duelling notebooks:

one tells the story, of a pulp log
journal writing truth as lies &
poems writing lies as truth; *which*
                    would you believe?

if she was ever blonde as blonde
or beautiful as she were quick
& brilliant sweet, if she were even she
or we were planting secrets
                    in the temple of her thighs

if I were even there or here, if I
were rapt in sex or even thirty-eight
years old, if seven years is long enough
to remember to forget, to grow
a new skin, new body waiting
                    writing in the margin

if I could fill these blanks
if I could fill these stories & these scars

if I could write these stars the
                    letters of her name

glow down upon her; the shade her
pudding-stone
                    , for *putting up*
          & such

parts of a doorframe

the whole world posits little

end of autumn / time
blooms forward

& stands down

if but running
could keep it available

[*sex at thirty-eight*]; forgotten
principle

of speech & writing, write
out a cavern

of another speech

what would happen
to a granary of snow

or softened fruit?

what would happen to the frame
if just a little light

could enter?

icon driven

I am content to leave my theory
; the baby w/ the bath

steps you & you & you & you
& you & beautiful restless you

an hour day would drop away
we are portable as clocks

these useless withered hands
at this point speculation

oh thousands of hands
w/ your playing cards more

than your prayer

how can I believe; even faith
a misnomer

tearing sex with whole heart

teasing sex out your tongue
& recreating it; like man

& a woman

writing out loose scriptures

[~~sex at thirty-eight~~] (a head count)

sex at sex at sex at sex at
sex at sex at sex at sex at
sex at sex at sex at sex at
sex at sex at sex at sex at
sex at sex at sex at sex at
sex at sex at sex at sex at
sex at sex at sex at sex at
sex at sex at sex at sex at
sex at sex at sex at sex at
sex at sex at

         thirty-eight years

     not   *thirty-eight times*

(more than)

(whos for counting)

collected

would be so joyous

a golden arch of knowledge; experience
& years, *of all the girls*

Ive loved, & loved
them all

mistaking heart for hole, mistaking
hole for the space in my head

less a collected than a sheer accumulation
of what body went before

, slowly fitting into the new

& what would make new,
renewed w/ my seventh letter

struck down by the seventh wave

as many years behind, begun

continued shield notes:

if this is anything
if this is canadian shield
          body north, pointed
& a bruised month, looking

for what comes next

if this is myth
if this is writing true or false
the lifeless land the lifeless rock
a moonscape uninhabitable
white men w/ guns go travel
          for lake trout mammal meat
come back to the train
come back south to suburb jobs & houses

if I am talking here
if this is even talk
the myth of women & men as they
          near their fortieth year
as forty the new thirty
as this is what Ive heard

as this is what Ive heard &
          want to believe

as a friend of mine turnd forty some
          seven years before, saying
no, no way; saying *cancel my birthday*

& taking three more than years to get over

suddenly I realize what silence is

the smell of the radiator, her
arm under pillow

if this her body exclamation mark
        a question I repeatedly ask
do you love me, do you love me
this continual; sex
at whatever age being

I am repeatedly my age

, percolation of willow, stone
& a stony silence

interchangeable between two volumes

this song, this smell I carry
further on into the world

elimination trance of quarters
marking too thin for stamps

& the letterhead

& a swift return address
I would translate a common noun

dissemination of some

would occupy the whole

signature event

against the signature
all else is transcribed

to a single writ
to a mark upon leaves

or a ripple

by losing this operation
the name itself derives

with/to whom I address

a traditional collapse
this love buckles under

such feeble narrative
& strategy

of art looking under

of subsequent these eyes

shirtless sleeves shape
what thinking residue

[~~sex at thirty-eight:~~] sure, steady breathing

if I am this
if I am such
if I am breath-body
if I am cloud
if I am mark upon
if I am skin made
if I am temperate
if I am bone & blood
if I am layered
if I am textured
if I am quick & the dead
if I am singular or multiple
if I am highway
if I am dross
if I am slow-mood & tempered
if I am supposing your other half
if I am completed
if I am conflicted
if I am porch-light
if I am modest compatible
if I am sure-footed, stepping
if I am carnal & unabashed
if I am all fingers for reading
if I am blind to this
if I am ageless
if I am the point that could map you
if I am the rose to your east
if I am entered against all numbers
& come through, come through

[~~sex at thirty-eight~~] (~~omission~~)

~~a poem written~~
~~single-sided on a train~~
~~out of a love~~
~~out of a loss~~
~~out of a longing for~~

~~what we are getting at~~

~~this sex at thirty-eight~~
~~this future~~
~~this poem of the future~~
~~& forestalling~~

~~how do you bring me~~
~~how do you sing me~~
~~sing~~
~~into the telephone~~
~~into these letters~~
~~into these absences~~
~~these omissions~~

~~every word I now write~~
~~has the hole of you hanging~~
~~over~~

~~hanging over me~~

[~~sex at thirty-eight:~~] perpetually begun

when I started this poem, writing sex
at thirty-eight; a north   anadia heat

writing into
& out of that north, letters
to my bombshell blonde, unfinished

every poem here would write you
every poem here begun, writing
       where are you & writing space
       where you & I would touch, begin

, begin again

in a european city writing your german roots
in the canadian north writing scottishness
      , this lack of speech

writing writing; where otherwise I would
entreaty be

& writing capreol, the payphones still
you never answer

where some would call not north
or north enough

[~~admitting out my borders~~]

writing-on-stone: [~~sex at thirty-eight~~]

how is this the poem it set out to be
or even close

this rock green moss companion
this perpendicular need

this mathematical certainty
numbers is as does; old kroetsch
twice my age, a poem

still evolving; [~~sex at thirty-eight,~~]
nights swoop very low; there can be no end

a percolation stone
of thinning branches; group of seven
tom thomson wild wet; *lake-swimming*

to know the depth eventually will surface
oh unfinished g I long to finish

slow & slow
w/in this flowering

w/in this unrelenting adaptation line & need

continued shield notes:

if this is where you begun
the poem is where we will continue

the poem of your 'nother, north

[~~writing sex at thirty-eight~~
~~writing how many more added~~]

I would repeat a noise
I would repeat a noise

I would harken back to

I am all the years we have already lived
riding geological formation, a survey

of what we had done
& have yet to do

[~~writing sex at thirty-eight~~]
writing out a universe on skin
held together tight w/ words

& wild cat-tails
& junction underbrush

I would embrace you, skin on skin
to ancient stone

& geophysical remain
; this cairn that you would paint me, on

the poem, heading south

write out impassible; *I planted a poem*
in the ground

& waited, spring, to see

if I am flightless as a sea-bird
if I am flightless as a broken line
    of prose

the hills would crumble, into

unnameable, unfinished, if I would meet you
somewhere passed between

what is a line a map
, protracted banner lines we sing
& flesh upon

the first time I saw you
the first time you spoke you radiated

warmth, a stone
warmth, the sunlit bowl of shale

reflecting outward; reflecting back
some ten

or tenfold, maybe more

the poem, taken root

[~~sex at thirty-eight:~~] political poem

the poem cant help but be political
, the space between two bodies

I hold out rich hand poor
& cant tell the difference

the train track & the tire tred
, a grade school margin of snow

, a ledger error, continued
down the snowy page

the birch lines black a horsehair brush
against widening blue

deplete the billowing smoke
amid the powerlines

the hills have eyes

the rolling cyprus hills
the rolling adirondacks

the rolling rocky folds
the rolling blue ridge spendour

the rolling snowy peaks
the rolling gatineau
the crisp precambian, up
      across the snowy backs

the poem folds
& then unfolds, furls

across the deep expanse
      of what else follows
against a primacy of parallel,
      north of fifty-four
against the stubble of a longer foot,
      that further bodies see

, remark upon
[; this business of sex]

; this margin of unfinished news

continued shield notes:

thrust a smokestack deep in hackled ground
& gasp

contingent smokestack rising; put it then,
a standing valley still

lateral the muscled earth

describes the ground the net worth possible,
a seed

as tall as it would creek & bleed

continued shield notes:

blood on the paper
blood in the water

blood on the tracks
lost in thirty-something idealism

bouncing off canadian shield

thunder bay
goose bay
horseshoe bay
parry sound
owen sound

if you could name the water
if you could wish it

black rock black rose black water

the sound on the page
writing any one thought out of another

writing poetry at the foot of
writing poem at the mouth
of the long river

writing when one will get home again
writing once bit, thrice shy
writing the end back out at the beginning

writing famous last words
writing live at the apollo
writing the cherry orchard

this accumulated flesh
[of sex;] this simple word

, this simple whorl

slow hand

what is
is a four letter word
come back to bleeding
at thirty-one, at thirty-eight
circumnavigating years
the seventh wave
the seventh seal
writing north as north
the pulp mulls prince george
the ontario mining booms & busts
the nickel held at arms length high
writing a penny for your thoughts
writing sex at
writing anything, noisy as a white river
writing phantoms at the only lake
writing lakes that dont exist
writing poem into statement into song
into floating entry
writing erotic & the mythic shelved
writing out this way, hopelessly devoted

continued shield notes:

the skeleton requirements attest
to work themselves carefully

barren at the land bare
echoes watch the water trace
& false play

mining & smelting works & then works
, grey pantomime of sludge

& whatever can grow as outcropped rock
& what cant; *another description*

the passing ships; you get out, then
you circle back

how many circles

moving forward ahead

[, ~~what sex~~

~~at thirty-eight;~~] it reads
the forest for the trees

Acknowledgements

Some of these poems have appeared as an above/ground press broadside, in the online journals *Otoliths* (Australia), *Dusie* (Switzerland), *Other Voices International* (California) & *Jacket* (Australia), & on the author's own blog, as well as the chapbook (both print & online) *sex at thirty-eight: letters to unfinished g.* (Ottawa ON/Edmonton AB: above/ground press, 2007). Thanks much to the editors & publishers involved. Thanks to Amanda Earl for her keen & kind editorial eye, and Karl Siegler, publisher *par excellence*, his patience, endurance & time.

Notes

"gifts": this section is dedicated to "the writers & the regulars" (in order): _____, Trineer, Graham, Reid, Mulligan, Derosie, Newlove, Coleman, Grantham & Sylliboy, Seguin-McLennan, Christakos, Lavery, Earl, Rhodes & Gowan, Desbarats, Dolman & Moran, Purkis, Seguin, beaulieu, Kennedy, Latremouille, Viduka & Brammall, Harding, McFadden, curry, Middle, Douglas, Wilson & Harris, Rowley, Torck, Hussey, Massey, Miller, O'Connor, McDonnell & Woods, Lee & Martin, O'Meara & Jeffreys, McLennan, Prevost, Stone, Zytveld & MacDonald-Zytveld, Watcham, Cation, Showler, Double, Zafiroudis, McElroy, Hodgson, Norris & Richards.

"~~sex at thirty-eight~~ unfinished shield notes: letters to g.": this piece has to thank Dennis Cooley, Robert Kroetsch, Karen Clavelle, Andy Weaver & Kelly Laycock, Stephen Brockwell, & Barry McKinnon for not only being there as a friend & general influence, but helping to start the whole series, for himself & for me, & for whoever else happened to be around at the time, doing those most essential & helpful things: *being themselves*. It is such as them who make the poetry *happen*. First draft written on the VIA Rail train from Winnipeg to Toronto, November 23–24, 2006. This poem knows whom it's for.